Dear Reader and Friend, my name is **Zornitsa Maleva-Zlateva**, a Psychologist, Family Constellations Facilitator and Writer.

This is my GIFT to you - my self-help book Parental Blessing.

I would really appreciate it if you read this book and to recommend it to a friend if you like what is written in it. I would also like to invite you to follow me on **YouTube.**

If you feel the book content has been helpful, and you can afford it, please donate **5.99 GBP** to my **Revolut** or **PayPal** so I can continue writing and printing this and other books (the donation is to cover my cost for transport and printing the book), and help others heal their life so they can have fantastic relationships with partners, family and friends!

I really appreciate your help and support! Thank you in advance.

With love and warm wishes.

Zornitsa

PayPal:

Zornitsa Maleva-Zlateva

Scan to pay Zornitsa Maleva-Zlateva

YouTube:

Parental Blessing
First edition, English, 2023

© Zornitsa Maleva, author
Cover illustration: Mira Doichinova
Editor: Snezhina Tsvetanova
Editor on English: Vaniya Angelova

Prepress: Katerina Valkova
Print: Direct Services Ltd.

Publisher: Zornitsa Maleva

ISBN: 978-619-92596-0-3
Sofia 2023

Zornitsa Maleva

Parental Blessing

2023

Only one person is needed to change your life here and now and that is YOU.

After reading this book, you will have everything you have dreamt of in your relationships – personal/partner relationships and parents-child-parents based bonds, just for 30 days.

Theory and practice based on Helinger's method and a self-help guide, and also a therapy in difficult and love-missing bonds in our relationships with the beloved person and in children-parents based relations.

You will find out why you did not have a partner beside you, and why it was difficult for you to build a relationship. After reading this book, you will have the relationship and the relations you have dreamt of here and now.

What will you learn from this book?

This book will change your life from good to your happy reality - here and now ... After reading this book, you will live in the vibration of love, you will easily attract love in your current relationships (marriage, partner's relationship). This book is dedicated to healing and improving relationships through constellations. Constellations are a method of healing the whole family system and returning the negative patterns of behavior, way of life, and beliefs to the person to whom they belong in the family thus releasing us completely from them. And we as the last ones who came to the family system, we do not have to pay for the mistakes of our ancestors. After obtaining this knowledge, with the techniques and rituals, you will be completely free to live your life filled with love, you will love and you will be loved. All dramas will disappear and if you do not have a partner, the best partner for you will enter your life. You will have children, you will find your mission and you will be the best version of yourself, the one you have dreamed of. Last but not least, after performing the Parental Blessing ritual, you will have complete reconciliation and acceptance of your parents as they are, like a mother and a father in your heart. Then, miracles will begin to happen one after another. This book will teach you how to connect with your ancestors and use their resources, strength, support, and how to open your heart to love.

Here you will find the ritual of obtaining a parental blessing. This is an ancient Slavic ritual that is very powerful. It allows us to connect with the family and unlock the flow of love for us in our family.

You will find formulas in times of great difficulties, to clear your way and to attract the good in your life. There are also Tibetan exercises and guidelines for what kind of a man/a woman you want to have in your life.

You will learn how to have the best relationship with your beloved person, how to have the man or woman of your dreams. You will understand what has prevented you from having love and what has stopped you from loving and being loved – here and now.

Here you will find invaluable advices for harmonious and loving relations between a man and a woman, in relationship and marriage.

You will understand how I received everything in my life with ease, only after one constellation and the blessing of my parents. And I know that this is the way, because I have confidently crossed my inner desert and recognized the path of love, and I want this for you as my readers.

Thank you for buying this book today! By reading it you will find out how to solve your problems related to relationships, whether personal or professional, and I am convinced that after reading the book you will become the best version of yourself and you will have a deeper insight about many aspects of your life. This system will change your life here and now. I have the feeling that you really interested in how to improve your life in all its aspects and you need guidance to do that.

I wish you to live in your happy reality – here and now, fulfilled and overflowing with the vibration of Love in all aspects of your life!

Let your happy reality begin today – here and now!

With all respect to you, my readers, with lots of love,

Zornitsa

Prologue

This book is dedicated to my Mom and Dad.

To you, my Readers.

To my Teachers, from whom I have learned so much and now I can share it with you.

To my beloved **Man**, without whose love and support this would not be a reality.

And I thank Myself for realizing and understanding the power of the family behind me and the blessings of my mom and dad ... now I feel complete and I know who I am.

The very moment we are conceived, this is the moment of the strongest love between the mother and the father. The greatest gift we get from our parents is life.

I will talk about the different kinds of blessings we can receive, even if our parents have died.

The blessing itself is so strong that it can strengthen and protect the family and the future generations - your children.

Our parents are the best parents we can have. I want to write this in capital letters. Your Mother and Father are just a man and a woman and have the right to have whatever relations they want to have between themselves. For us, as children, there is a place after them.

We should never forget that there is a hierarchy in family.

I will discuss this issue in the book and how violating this hierarchy leads to a lot of entanglements and problems - financial, personal, etc.

Contents

Parental blessing consists of four parts. This is a ritual for self-help and complete reconciliation with our parents on a spiritual level. This opens our heart for love and enables us to be happy and loved by our partner, the people around us, so that we love, create and preserve these loving relationships in our lives.

Meditation is the key, if we are alone, to meet and attract the man or woman of our life – here and now. After performing this ritual, on a spiritual level, we become happier with our parents and allow ourselves to live our lives through love – here and now. There is no exception. Here, this works for all because we all have parents who are part of our family.

5.4. How to ask for a blessing from your mother and father in the Good Letter? – Fourth part

6. Prayers and formulas for attracting love, abundance, harmony, success and personal protection against bad influences and people in our lives

7. Some advices for harmonious and loving bonds between a man and a woman in relationship/marriage

8. How do we understand what partner we want and is he/she the right person for us in our lives?

9. The Tree of Desires

10. Parental Blessing - the seminar that will change your life – here and now

11. How do I love myself, my parents and the person beside me healthily?

12. Who am I?

1. For me and my path in awareness

My dear readers,

I write this book for you to share my experience as a family constellation facilitator and to help as much as I can to make your life better each day. As reading my story and my experience with constellations you will understand why my mission became helping people through family constellations. Thank you for buying this book today!

Here you will find out how to solve your problems related to relationships, whether personal or professional, and I truly believe that after reading this book you will be the best version of yourself, you will receive deeper insight about many aspects of your life. This system will change your life – here and now. I have the feeling that you are really interested in how to improve your life in all aspects, and you need a little bit of guidance to do this – here and now. That is why I share my knowledge with you, because I want the best for you as my readers.

I was born wise and beautiful. I sincerely thank my dad Dimitar and my mom Dobrinka for everything they gave me as my parents, and it is so much.

I found my path, which is: healing the soul through family constellations.

But before I came to this awareness, my path was connected with a lot of pain and family drama. It took me a lot of searching, time, knowledge and energy until I came to the simple truth that everything in this life is related to the fact that we owe nothing to our parents, and we are solely responsible for our own deeds, actions and choices in life, which we consciously make each day.

I really do understand how you feel when reading these words. I felt the same way, and many people do feel the same way every day - they feel obligated to their parents. The loyalty to our parents at the subconscious level is so great that we often prefer to be "good" for mom and dad as children rather than being good to ourselves as individuals. This, to such an extent, entangles the order and hierarchy in the family system that it often leads to anger, pain, anxiety and disappointment. Most often at the subconscious level we burden the person next to us with these feelings, and we suppress them to our parents. And if we see something that slightly reminds us of a trait or behaviour typical to our parents, something that had hurt us as children, we tend to be rude to our husband/wife, to our partner beside us. We do not set limits clearly marking the line up to where our parents can interfere with our lives and our new partner's family.

How sad, and that's the reality of so many people.

And here is what I have discovered, after a lot of searching and wandering, that's important to me.

For a long time, I thought my parents were obliged to do this or that for me - to love me just as I wanted to, but then I realized they were just human beings, not gods. They are just a man and a woman who will live their lives as they want and have the right to make their own mistakes. Their personal life as a man and a woman is not my job. I am just a child, and they are adults. OH, HOW TERRIBLY DIFFICULT IT WAS FOR ME not to be the mother and father of my parents, not to preach them: "You see, I know better, my way is the right one", but just to let me be a child and accept them as they are in my heart, without correcting or condemning them.

It took me three full years, with a lot of work as a personal progress, and my meeting with the constellations. That changed everything. My whole perception of the world, family and life has changed for good.

Because if we do not live our mission, our partner can not make us happy, nor can our children be able to fill our own gaps. The strong love of our mother and father, when we are conceived, gives us the strength. The same is with our bonds with the ancestors behind us. I will discuss this in a separate chapter later on in the book, "How to open our hearts to them, our parents, without pain and without fear of condemnation and rejection". And yes, it is possible to happen - here and now. For you to be completely happy. Once I have succeeded, you will succeed too. I am fully convinced of what I say here, because I have experienced it and I am living the life of my wildest dreams now. I want this for you as my readers.

I will start from the very beginning, from my childhood. The example I'm going to give is pretty dramatic and shocking, but it's real. It's part of my life. I will start by telling that I had an independent and carefree childhood in the village. Somewhere until my eighth year, nobody required much from me as a child, mainly to study my lessons. We are three children from the constellation point of view and I'm the middle child. I have an older brother and a younger sister. I grew up in a village with lots of love and care from my parents, as well as from my grandparents. But I had not realized this until recently, because I lived through the pain and trauma of my childhood as a result of my parents' separation when I was two years old.

We were living, my mother, my sister and my grandparents, in a house in the village. The pain of my mother from the divorce transferred to me and out of loyalty to her, I have chosen, with my child's understanding at that time, not to meet with my father and to be the "good child" in my mother's eyes. From the constellation point of view, I stopped being my mother's child, and I was trying to take on the place of my father by emotionally supporting her. However, it was an impossible task for me for I was just a little child. I grew up with a huge gap inside of me as the feeling of my missing father was getting stronger. At some point, I began to say that my father had died. Many of my relatives supported this lie, and I accepted it as normal, and I began to believe strongly in it. Not understanding that I do not have to choose between my parents, I lived with this perception until my 25th year.

I grew up, I became a student and got enrolled to study in Sofia. I did not like what I was studying, but my mother was so happy and so proud of me that I continued to study this with reluctance. I went on like this until the second year of my studies. Then, I moved from home, and I rented an apartment. It was hard for me, but I felt free. I began to read the writings of Petar Danov. I came upon The Alchemic and decided that I wanted to run away from my mother, somewhere far away. I did not sit for my final examinations just to "punish" her. At least that was what I thought at that moment. Then I moved to study in UK Events Management and that was what I wanted to do.

When I was leaving, my mother said I did not have mother anymore until I take my final examinations. I answered "Okay" and I left. I was thinking, "I'll show her how it is done. I know it".

I graduated. I was alone on my graduation in UK and I was very sad because I achieved so much, and there was no one to see it. My grandfather was very happy for me.

The saddest part was that I could not build a good and complete relationship with a man. This was due to the strong fear and pain of not being hurt and abandoned. That's why I always hurt first and I ran away. I always ran and hurt first.

I met my current husband and again the same scenario. But this time, the man beside me was really there and loved me. I was afraid of the moment that any of my relatives could tell him that my father was alive, the lie was between us. I found out that I needed help and then I started therapy.

I was filled with a lot of anger directed to my father, but I did not know how to express it and I projected this anger in my relationships. I remember that I did not trust men and I punished them because I missed my father. It was hard for me to have a normal and real relationship. I preferred to build walls around myself so that no one could hurt me. With time, seeing other couples who shared intimacy, trust and love, I started telling myself that there was obviously another way of communication and that I had to find out how that was working. Then my path to personal growth began. I bought most of the self-help books I managed to find in the bookshop at that time. But these books gave no explanation of the importance of the mother and father in our lives. I went to see a psychologist, but that did not help. Then the pain remained. I concentrated on work and my studies, and time passed on. Until the day, when by accident or not, I found myself at a personal growth seminar that discussed the importance of the parents. It was my first introduction to constellations. After the first session, the therapist told me I should go and meet with my father, otherwise she could not work with me, and I had to look for another therapist if I wanted to. She gave me a one-week deadline to do that. Before I went, we worked on my anger and I visited a constellation seminar. SHE GAVE ME ONE WEEK TO DO IT.

From this day on, my life was not the same. Everything has changed after my meeting with my father. My homework, after the seminar, was to go and visit my father after more than 20 years. The last time I had seen him was when I was a child, and now I had to go there.

Before I went, I wrote the "Letter of Anger", in which I poured down on paper all the pain and anger I kept towards him. Then, I wrote the "Good Letter", which also concerned the secret that I was saying that he had died. I had to give this letter to him personally when I visited him. These two letters are an ancient Tibetan method for healing the pain – natural and simple method to reconcile the level of the souls from children to parents, from woman to man, etc. This is so simple and so effective. Feeling the power of the method, I realized how long I had lived in emptiness, and now I was whole and complete. I felt free and loved by my parents.

I remember the moment I rang the bell on my father's door. There was so much emotions and thoughts rambling in my head. "Well, if he does not open the door, if he tells me he does not want to see me ..." The child's fear deep in me projected different outcomes without it being my reality.

The door slightly opened... My father looked at me and cried out with joy that he was seeing me.

He embraced me. I had been waiting this embrace for so long. I felt strength, warmth, love and protection from my dad.

(And in my mind, he did not love me and did not want me – this was the fantasy of the inner hurt child). He told me about my grandparents. I learnt that my great-grandfather was a doctor's assistant, a very respected and loved person in the city. I saw my baby picture on the cupboard...

My dad said, "I've been waiting for you each day, my child, and I love you very much". I returned from that meeting – like another person. I just have realized how much I missed him and how I searched for him in all the men around me. My husband also noticed the change - as if I were another woman.

I got angry at my mother, and I blamed her in my heart. The therapist I was working with told me about the constellations and she offered me the chance to attend the sessions of such a group. She explained to me that the result would be much better, and her work finished here.

So, this is how my journey with my constellations began and my development as a facilitator and coach.

If I had to be honest, at first, I thought these people were nuts, they gathered round in a circle, they talked about their ancestors, and I just waited the session to finish so that I could leave until my turn in the group came and I sat down on the chair.

The constellator radiated love and tranquillity. He listened to me and said, "You will not be the same person. Things will find the right place in your heart, you will see". The constellation itself was very emotional and strong for me. There I reconciled with my mother and father. It felt like a backpack full of stones has fallen off my shoulders right there. I opened my heart for my parents. I could love and be loved. I finally figured out what it was to trust and open to love. I saw my parents as they were. I realized that they did the best they could with the resources they had at that time.

This changed my relations with my husband and the people around me. My life has changed for good. Now, when I have everything, I want to share this with you, because the method of "family constellations" really does miracles for the soul through the essence of human being. I do not know if there is another so simple and effective method. Seeing the positive results, I decided to receive training from the best family constellation facilitator. This is a two-year training course that includes 6 semesters, with ongoing work with internal traumas and a lot of knowledge.

I am grateful to God, myself, and my parents for choosing this path - to help people, for I confidently walked through my emotional desert, realizing that the path is through LOVE. And here I am now, in front of you, I share all this with my heart open because I want the best for you, my clients and readers - here and now. Tomorrow may be too late. Change begins with you, today - here and now. The techniques provided in this book will change your life today.

My mission, through the constellations and self-healing techniques, is to see you satisfied, happy and open to the channel of love, harmonious and loving relationships filled with abundance in life.

With sincere respect to all of you, my clients, and readers,
Be blessed!
Your ... ZORNITSA

You can contact me through my Facebook page: Zornitsa Maleva – Family Constellations. Each "Like" on my Facebook page will give you free sample info of my couching sessions and seminars.

You can contact me through my YouTube channel: Relationship Coaching for you with Zornitsa Maleva

Website: zornitsamaleva.com

2. The power of the genus and why it is important to know where we come from

Who are we?

Few of us know the history of their ancestors and the history of their family. In the following lines I will explain why this is important...

When working with constellations, we recognize the family as a living family tree in which all our ancestors up to the seventh generation behind us, are directly related to us, the heirs (the children, the grandchildren). There is no exception here. As a rule, the last person who came to the family (grandson/ granddaughter) pays for the mistakes of the grandmother/ great-grandmother, grandfather/ great-grandfather. This is because all the members of a given family tree are connected through the so-called "morphogenetic field" or the field of knowledge. It collects information about all the pains, murders, betrayals, and frauds that a representative of the family has done while he was alive. Also, a certain member of the family can also be considered as a resource for that family, if he has done something big and good that the family is proud of. We are directly related to our parents and grandparents through subconscious loyalty. We very often become its victim, and that prevents us from living our life as it is, without being entangled with the fate of a member of the family we represent, without knowing and wanting this ourselves. In most cases, these are people having a difficult fate and we have the so-called "entanglement" with them, with the persons excluded from the system. This "entanglement" can be removed during constellation. As Hellinger says, "there is an invisible accounting book that records all accounts between family members and family".

In constellations, we recognize the family itself as a system in which every single member, seven generations back on the mother and father line, has a definite place and no one under any circumstances can take their place. If this happens, gaps and entanglements appear in the system, and this leads to problems in our lives. We have the right to live our destiny. Each one's destiny is unique and belongs to the individual, however hard and difficult may that destiny be. And only that very person can and should live it.

Very often, violations in a system occur when a member of that system decides to help another member of the system, violating this simple rule that we can not interfere and change the fate of our relative because we are no bigger than Fate and God. The only thing we can do is to live our lives in their honour - with respect to those who came before us (our ancestors and parents) and to do our best. This, in most cases, is enough so that the flow of harmony and love flows through the system. There are two types of conscience in the family system. The Good conscience means that one is sure he/she belongs to the system, and the Bad conscience means that one is afraid of being excluded from his/her system. I will provide more details on this issue in the chapter about the Laws of Love that are directly related to us and our family, determining whether we will have difficulties in life or we will live harmoniously - here and now.

2.1 Exercise to strengthen the support of our ancestors to us

This is a very powerful and effective exercise that helps when we lack strength and have difficulties in our life. Imagine how effective it is because we have the power and experience of our ancestors behind us and their support.

1. Please sit comfortably on a chair and close your eyes. Breathe in and breathe out three times.

2. Lean back on the chair and put your feet on the ground. Let them be relaxed and touch the floor with your feet. The hands are relaxed on both sides of the body.

3. Imagine how your father put a hand on your right shoulder, behind him is your grandfather, who put his hand on your father's right shoulder. Behind him is your great-grandfather, he put his hand on your grandfather's right shoulder, and continue up to the seventh generation back in the family. You are the first generation.

4. Now imagine your mother who puts her hand on your left shoulder. Behind her stands your grandmother who puts a hand on your mother's left shoulder. Behind her is your great-grandmother who puts a hand on your grandmother's left shoulder and continues up to seventh generation. You are the first generation.

5. Now, we must check where in the system we feel uncomfortable (right at that very place there exist entanglements and violations of the Laws of Love), you do the following: For the first generation, you take the thumb that represents ourselves and press it strongly against the little finger, while at that moment you imagine your father. If you have an unpleasant feeling, fear, or some indisposition, you stay like that a little bit to connect with the field of knowledge, you remember the feeling and then continue with all fingers up to fifth generation. Or to the great-great-grandfather. You work with the right hand for men (that is, our fathers and grandfathers) and with the left hand for women (that is the relationship with our mothers and grandmothers). Please give about one minute to each finger, to each hand.

6. When you finish the exercise, you record all the unpleasant feelings and put down on a sheet of paper in details what you have experienced with each generation. This helps a lot. Then when you make your constellation, you can quickly remove the blockages precisely and effectively, without making guesses.

7. You end the exercise by getting up from the chair and shaking your body. You tap yourself on your face and say your name: I am .... It is very important to do ...

8. The last step is done in order not to get entangled and is a mandatory ending part of the exercise. You should not improvise. Just follow strictly the steps to get results.

2.2 Generating a genogram

What does the "genogram" represent and why should we do a genogram in order to start the healing effect of the system?

The genogram is some kind of a family tree that contains information up to 7 generations back to your mother's and your father's line. It includes certain facts that allow the client to see and realize family bonds, as well as their belonging to the system or the family he/she comes from. As I explained previously in the book, our family is recognized as a system. Now we shall take a more detailed look on how the family is recognized from a constellation's point of view. Each of us, as a representative of our family, belongs to the family consisting of our parents and ancestors and a current, actual family. Our parents are our family by birth – my mother, father and me, my brothers and sisters, and all the ancestors behind us. We look at them up to the seventh generation on our mother's and father's line. This includes the living and deceased brothers and sisters, us and our parents. Aborted children, early-deceased children, and all family members whom the family is ashamed of and whom the family members do not talk about, such as sick children, people who have left the family, someone in prison, murderers, or those with psychological disorders. Here we include our aunts and uncles on father's and mother's line, without the cousins.

Our current, actual family is a separate family. It includes me and my partner/ husband/ wife and our children. This also includes any live, deceased, aborted children, miscarried childbirth, the children who left the family. Children born in previous marriages and from other partners. It needs to be clarified if any of the spouses in the current family had a serious relationship or marriage before the wedding and what was the reason for the separation without going into details. It needs to know if there were any tragic events related to this family. This also applies to the parent family. Building the genogram is a complicated process and takes time. Meaning, this family will continues the genus. Mom and Dad have no place in this family on either side. If they interfere, this causes a violation in the system and we pay the price for it.

The genogram could show that for several generations back in time, the first child has always died at birth or that there are repetitive situations in several generations. You may even find that marriages have happened the same way. For example, men always marry an older woman on a certain date, and that's not accidental. At Parental Blessing seminar, we will work in details on building the genogram. Here, I will give some guidelines on making a simple genogram. The most important condition is that you have thoroughly questioned your parents about them and their parents, about your grandparents. Also, if they have died and you cannot obtain this information, you should contact your relatives trying to receive such information from relatives, aunts and uncles, by writing down everything they tell you.

Sometimes, even the very drawing of the genogram brings a tremendous benefit to the client, as he/she has an opportunity to discover their family's history and see systemic violations. The facts and events that happened to your family members, not the personality of the people, are important. The sequence of dates and events is important.

What information is needed for making up client's genogram?

1. All sisters and brothers of the client, half-sisters and half-brothers, if the situation is one mother and two fathers, one father and two mothers;

2. Stepbrothers and stepsisters, adopted children;

3. Client's own children;

4. Father and mother, including foster parents – father and mother;

5. Aunts and uncles, excluding cousins;

6. Grandparents on the mother's and father's side;

7. All birthdays, as well as dates of death;

8. Divorce / separation dates;

9. Stay in a prison or a psychiatric clinic of any family members;

10. Previous partners of parents;

11. Previous partners of grandparents;

12. Have parents been forced to marry just because of pregnancy;

13. Have grandparents been forced to marry just because of pregnancy;

14. Diseases, including hereditary diseases;

15. Still-born children and abortions;

16. Early deceased family members;

17. Severe incidents, including murder or suicide of a family member, even back in time in the system up to 7 generations;

18. Left children or children given for raising by other people, relatives, orphanage institutions...;

19. Financial failures and successes;

20. Sexual abuse;

21. Family secrets and taboo issues in the family;

22. Historical events – such as emigration, wars, exits, political situations and others;

23. Cases of exclusion of members out of the system, the so-called "black sheep";

24. Religious and ethnic belongings;

25. "The Saints" in the family system;

26. Cases of mysterious death or death not mentioned because it is very difficult and painful.

The family constellation can not work accurately and precisely, without the information from the client's genogram and a detailed interview on the existence of a family exclusion.

How a genogram is made?

The figure presented here by following the rule "the women on the left, the men on the right" starts from the last members, meaning from you, and goes back to 6 generations of great-grandmothers and great-grandfathers.

3. The Laws of Love by Bert Hellinger and why, if we break them, nothing good is expected in our life?

FIRST LAW OF LOVE

The principle of hierarchy and seniority in the system reads as follows: Greater systemic importance have those who came before us in family: Great-grandfather – grandfather – father – son; Great-grandmother – grandmother – mother – daughter

There is no exception to that rule! And if we think we are more important, we do not respect those who came before us, and nothing good is expected in our lives. The following rule without any exception applies here:

We should not interfere in our parent's personal life and we should not save our parents! We are just children, and they are the adults and they can deal with the problems in life. We should concentrate on our lives and accept the fate of our parents as it is – showing respect. We are no greater than Fate or God to interfere and save them!

The following points are important here: we do not give them money, advice, we do not take sides in conflicts, because if we do, we take on the role of parents and they become children and the order is confused. Then problems will start for both sides. We do not live with our parents and do not let them interfere with our private life too much, but why?

Our parents are our birth family. This family consists of my mother, father, me and my brothers and sisters (with all the ancestors behind us).

The present family is another separate family. It includes me and my partner as well as our children. This family includes any live and deceased children, aborted children as well as miscarried children, adopted children and children born from other marriages and relationships of one or the other partner. This family continues the genus.

The mother and the father (our parents) on both sides have no place in this family. If we do not set boundaries and accept the fact that our parents are just parents, but not our friends or partners in our present family, this is a violation according to the Law of Hierarchy, and we shall pay our price. Here happens the so-called "entanglement" or identification with a parent or an ancestor in our lives without understanding it. In case of too much interference by our parents, at the energy level, a family constellation for removing of the entanglement is made. Children do this out of loyalty on the energy level and often take the place of a missing parent or someone excluded from the system by following the principle "Better me than you, I will follow you even in death". Meaning, we have a recurrence of diseases and repeated unfortunate events without understanding why.

THERE IS ONLY ONE EXCLUSION. IT IS ONLY IF THE PARENTS ARE SERIOUSLY ILL. THEN WE HELP, BUT WE SHOULD DO THIS WITH HIGHEST RESPECT TO THEIR FATE.

SECOND LAW OF LOVE – THE RIGHT OF BELONGING TO THE SYSTEM

No one should not be and can not be excluded from the system. Each member of the system has a specific place in it. There must be no secrets and any refusal to talk about ancestors, or of any member of the system. For example, if someone has done something bad and the members of the system are ashamed of that person – no one spokes about the person; a murder and someone is in jail; an abortion - no one wants to talk about this child just because of the pain; a birth of an extra-marital child - the parents chase away the daughter; a rape - shame of the son. This leads to consequences such as the inability to hold a partner and impossibility to have a child, cheating, etc.

Facts from the family history are important for family constellations. We just see things as they are in the system of the particular person. Family constellation is based on the facts as they are to see where the system has been broken and why (cracked by a disconnected person). These violations directly affect us, the CHILDREN in the form of diseases and anxiety.

THIRD LAW OF LOVE - THE BALANCE OF GIVE AND TAKE

This is may be the most important law!

• Giving from parents to children - It goes like this: Parents give love, protection, time, money and food unconditionally to their children until they are 18 years old. Then, children become parents and start giving the same to their children unconditionally. This is normal and natural. Children accept with love and respect all that their parents want and can give them.

• Giving by a friend to a friend in equal relation - "We give equal to have friendship". If one gives more, the friendship breaks down or the person disappears. There are no exceptions here!

• Giving from a beloved partner to the other partner, and vice versa. Here one partner gives, then the other partner gives a little more and so the relationship grows and develops. I DO NOT TALK ONLY FOR MONEY HERE AS GIVING. If one partner only gives and the other partner only takes, such relationships are doomed to failure because the relationship takes the "child-parent" model.

I BELIEVE THAT YOU UNDERSTAND THE IMPORTANCE OF THIS INFORMATION AND NOW THERE IS NO EXCUSE FOR YOU THAT YOU DO NOT UNDERSTAND HOW YOUR ACTS CREATE YOUR FUTURE AND THE FUTURE OF YOUR CHILDREN!

3.1. When we have deceased parents, we work by using a chair or another object, crouching with respect and honour, as if the parent is in front of you. All rituals are being performed again, in the same way. They shall end with the words: "You have a special place in my heart, I respect you, you are not forgotten, and I will live my life in your honour, in the best way".

4. What a constantation is and why should I use it in my life?

My dear readers,

I write this book for you to share my experience of a family constellation and to help as much as I can to make your life better each day.

I will start by explaining what a constellation is.

Constellation is a three-dimensional, group process that represents a family system or a live family tree of a certain person. It includes all ancestors and relatives, where each one having a definite place in the system and no one can be excluded. In family constellation, hidden things come to light, for example, conflicts and destructive relationships, and the system seeks compensation for injustice. Those persons excluded from the system, in one way or another, must be returned so that love can flow freely between its members. Most often, the youngest member of the system or the last member of the system (the children – granddaughter, grandson, etc.) pay the price. During a constellation, it is possible to resolve these conflicts and return those who have been forgotten or excluded for some reason from the family system. That is, everyone should take their place by rank and hierarchy in the system. The so-called "family ranking by hierarchy" is made.

GREAT-GRANDMOTHER – GRANDMOTHER – MOTHER- DAUGHTER – GRANDDAUGHTER

GREAT-GRANDFATHER – GRANDFATHER – FATHER – SON – GRANDSON

The examples of exclusion in a family system are as follows:

• Divorce – The child lives with one parent and nobody is talking about the other parent. The child is in put into the situation of choosing between his/her mother and father and carries the pain that is not his/hers, hating one of the parents, depending on the situation.

• Abortion – An abortion was made and nobody is talking about this child as if they never existed. (If this child is not recognized in the system this shall lead to breakdown of the relationship between the partners, and that is the price paid if what happened is rejected)

• Early death of children – Mainly, speaking of our grandmothers, this has usually happened very often and leads to a loss of money and a lack of abundance in the family.

Here, I will also help with a powerful ritual and constellation, and then everything comes in to place.

The facts and events that happened to the members of your family are important, not the personality of the people!

Questions that are asked before constellation are valid for both your mother's family and your father's father, looking back in time to the sixth generation of great-grandmother and great-grandfather. We are searching for the reasons of death for each family member, and if there are any strange events in your family like:

• Early death – we search for a person in your mother's and/or father's family deceased under the age of 25 years;

• Whether in your family someone remained without parents under the age of 25 years. Especially important here is death occurred during or after birth, even if it was your great-grandmother.

Other events may include suicides or suicide attempts; crimes, especially murders; someone who has been deceived, for example by inheritance, a promise of marriage, which was given, but not kept, etc.; difficult fate or accidents; someone has been stigmatized or expelled from the family; illegal children born or children who have been abandoned; A soldier or a person killed during wars (great-grandfather or grandfather); Adopted children; Drug addiction and alcoholism;Abuse and violence; Secrets in the family; Parallel relationships, cheating; Did our parents have previous matrimonial relationships, fiancès and previous marriages, as well as any mixed marriages.

Unfortunately, all this affects us directly, as the heirs, and we, as the last generation came into the family, pay a hard price for the actions of our parents. It sounds cruel, but it is the fact, however, with constellation it can be healed and returned to the person to whom it belongs by being acknowledged and accepted in our heart with love. Only then can we live our life here and now, and be the person we are.

PROBLEMS VERY OFTEN ARISE IN OUR LIVES MAINLY BECAUSE OF:

1. BAD RELATIONS WITH OUR PARENTS

2. NOT ACCEPTING IN OUR HEARTS OUR PARENTS AS THEY ARE - A MAN AND A WOMAN

3. REJECTING THE FACT THAT OUR PARENTS ARE ENTITLED TO MAKE MISTAKES AND THEY ARE JUST HUMAN BEINGS

4. REJECTING THEIR HIERARCHY, THE FACT THAT IN TERMS OF RANKING THEY COME BEFORE US AS OUR PARENTS

5. "Parental Blessing" – The ritual that will change your life here and now

"Parental Blessing" in IV parts

What is a "Parental Blessing" and why is it so important to us, the children?

The detailed performance and the ritual are provided to the clients, during the "Parental blessing" seminar. While performing this, each one of you can feel the power of this ritual. It needs to be performed by a group and representatives of your mother and father. But there is a way for this ritual to be performed on its own, without a facilitator. The formulas that are used for duration of this ritual are very ancient and have an exceptionally healing action on you. It helps you to reconcile with yourself, to protect the defenceless child within and to feel the strength and support of your parents and ancestors.

The dates for the seminar can be found on my Facebook page. Everyone who purchases this book receives a lot of information and advice on harmony.

Very often, we, as children, carry within a deep insult from our parents. We forget that they are just a man and a woman, not just parents, and have the right to live their lives as they wish, and we have the right to live our lives the way that we want.

„Parental blessing" is a deep internal process in which „holes are filled" and one excluded from the system take their proper place. You, as a child, you leave completely free of old patterns, and miracles start to happen in your life, because the love channel begins to flow freely. This is a deep, group, meditational constellation, with a powerful healing and therapeutic effect for a life that is better, harmonious and full of love and material benefits. And the most important part is that we heal traumas where your parents (mother and father) take their place in your heart and everything in your life is already happening with ease. My life has changed radically after this ritual, and I want the best for you, my clients and readers – here and now.

I will provide part of the ritual, which can be performed by itself, only by yourselves, without your parents having to attend while you perform it.

For those of you who have a good relationship with your parents, please **do the following**. Ask your mother/father to put a hand on your head. Kneel, showing your respect to her/him and ask her/him to bless you and your children with theirs own words. This is also a healing act.

Unfortunately, our parents also carry many traumas and can not be completely neutral. They are just people and just for giving us life, we have to find a place in our heart for them and be grateful and respectful.

Sometimes, our parents must be loved from a distance but never to exclude them from our heart and family. In the previous chapter I explain in detail the Laws of Love and how they can help in our lives.

5.1 Meditation for reconciliation with parents – First part

„Parental blessing" – a self-help ritual in cases of having poor or missing close relationships with our parents.

This ritual helps to fully restore harmony and spiritual relationships with our parental family, connecting and absorbing forces and support from the ancestors before us, properly aligning the hierarchy in the family and the family system. It also helps to open the space of love and the building of our own family with our own children, the continuation of a strong and happy family in which love is manifested in all its forms and flows freely among the members of the family system. This ritual helps to leave all the hurt of those belonging to the family system so that we can live our own lives in the best possible way - here and now, not that of our parents or grandparents.

This exercise is according to Bert Helinger and has a tremendous therapeutic effect for you.

You record this with your voice and listen to it once for 60 consecutive days. It has a tremendous therapeutic effect and heals pain from difficult childhood and difficult relationships with parents - divorced parents, missing parents, diseased parents, powerfully imposing parents, busy or always working parents. In addition, you reconcile completely, on internal level with your mothers and fathers, thus also becoming better parents for your own children. Even if you have a good relationship with your parents, this exercise will strengthen and encourage your relationship with them. I strongly recommend it to people who have difficulty keeping relationships, who are not married and have no children but would like to have, as well as for people who have difficulty in dealing with their partner and want more harmonious, monogamous relationships. It is to be done every week for 90 days.

Meditation for reconciliation with parents
Dear Mom/Mother,
I accept everything that comes from you,
all of it, with all the consequences.
I accept it at the price you have paid
and which I have paid for.
I will do something good from this, in your honour,
as a sign of gratitude and honour ...
What you did would not have been in vain.
I keep it in my heart
and if I'm allowed, I'll pass it on -
as you did.

I accept you as my mother
and you have me as your son/daughter.
You are my only mother and I am your child.
You are the older one and I am the younger one.
You give, and I receive, dear mother.
I'm glad you have chosen Daddy as your husband.
You are both the right parents for me.

Dear Father/Dad,
I accept everything that comes from you,
all of it, with all the consequences.
I accept it at the price you have paid
and which I have paid for.
I will do something good from this, in your honour,
as a sign of gratitude and honour ...
What you did would not have been in vain.
I keep it in my heart
and if I'm allowed, I'll pass it on -
as you did.
I accept you as my father
and you have me as your son/daughter.
You are my only father and I am your child.
You are the older one and I am the younger one.
You give, and I receive, dear father.
I'm glad you have chosen my Mother as your wife.
You are both the right parents for me.

This is the first part of the meditation ritual. Now, we will make the second part that breaks the old models we bring from our birth family so that we can live our lives as we want it without restrictions – here and now.

5.2. Second part of the "Parental blessing" ritual

Take 2 chairs and place them on the ground in front of you by placing them on the left (for your mother) and on the right (for your father) respectively.

Sit comfortably on the floor and close your eyes. Imagine that your mother and father are in front of you. They look at you with love and pride. Now, while preserving this state, please kneel with respect to your parents. Bow first to your mother by saying, „Dear Mother, thank you for my life and for choosing to have me!" Stay in this position for a few seconds.

Now, bow to your father (to the right where the chair is) and say, „Dear Father, thank you for my life and for choosing my Mother as your wife and choosing to have me as your child. Stay in this position for a few seconds.

Record this part with your own voice and listen to it with respect and honor to your parents. Play the record of the text, the blessing, and imagine that your mother and father bless you and tell you this, while you kneel before them, and they put their hand on your head with love and protection, saying:

Dear daughter/son, (your Mother says to you)
I bless you, with all of my tenderness, femininity and maternal love. Let love run in your life freely, each and every day. May you have reciprocity, tenderness and understanding with the person next to you. May you have children born with ease, healthy and strong, may you strengthen the love, trust and reciprocity with every generation ahead. And so the strength of the family will stand strong for infinity, for you and your future generations. You are the younger one, and I am the older one. We stand behind you , the women from the family,

we support you and your children. I wish you to live in your happy infinity and your thoughts to create your happy reality, creating a healthy and loving family here and now. I let you love with all your heart and I want you to be happier than myself. Face your sexuality, enjoy it by taking and giving. I have also allowed myself to be a woman. I break all negative patterns from the past and you remain completely free of them. This is to be done by the older ones and I will take care of this. I want you only to be happy and to follow your way as you wish. You have my support and approval. You do not owe me anything. I am proud of you as my child. I chose to have you and I am happy to be your Mother. Be blessed with my maternal love. It will keep you from harm and protect you in life, as an invisible shield, each and every day. My dear child, I love you. Your loving mother. You are allowed to look at your father with your own eyes. What happens to your father is between us. We will always be your parents.

Dear daughter/son, (your Father says to you)

I bless you with all my male power, protection and fatherly love. Let love run in your life freely and may you realize yourself professionally. May you develop the will in your life each and every day. I give you from my male power, and by connecting with the men of my family, I bless you to be strong, confident and successful in life. I believe in you and I know that you will surpass me and my family by your achievements and successes. I am beside you and I support you. I break all negative patterns from the past and you remain completely free of them. This is to be done by the older ones and I will take care of this. I want you only to be happy and to follow your way as you wish. You have my support and approval. You do not owe me anything. I am proud of you as my child. I chose to have you and I am happy to be your Father. Be blessed with my fatherly love, strength and protection. It will keep you from harm and protect you in life, as an invisible shield, each and every day. My dear child, I love you. Your loving Father. You are allowed to look at your mother with your own eyes. What happens to your mother is between us. We will always be your parents. May the power of the men of my family stand strong in your children and my they take the best of the men before us. They are there, and I, we both support you in your life.

The father looks at the daughter and says:

– As I look at you, I see your mother. Her beauty and femininity have passed to you. You are connected to the femininity and support of women in your generation. Be blessed, my daughter!

The mother looks at her son and says:

– As I look at you, I see your father, his strength and support, his strong will, the power of the man. You are connected with the male power of the men in your family. Be blessed, my son!

Always the little ones come in with respect to the elder ones, never the other way around!

With this, the ritual ends. We accept with gratitude these words of blessings from our parents to us, with respect in our hearts. This ritual is performed with full respect and gratitude to the ancestors. I recommend using chairs and kneeling before them. It makes you feel that you are small, and they are big, and that's good because it is the truth that you are a child for your parents. Allow yourself to love them without judging them, and just accepting them in your heart, by reconciling with them.

This ritual has a tremendous healing effect on the inner child so that it can take its place and we will be just children for our parents. Then the energies are arranged and we start to live our lives, filled with love, abundance and success.

Without having reconciled with our parents, in our hearts, our chances of having a successful relationship, a good career and realization are quite small. The system seeks balance so that the energy of love flows freely.

5.3. How do we release the anger towards our mother and father in the Letter of Anger?

This is a ritual for healing the pain we feel towards our parents and our family. It has a very powerful effect on improving the relationship with our parents and the family behind us, as well as for the healing the "inner child". The ritual is effective even if our parents have died, even if they do not want to communicate with us or for some reason, we are not in close relationship with them. Even if we have wonderful relationships with our parents, I recommend that you perform this ritual. After performing the ritual, the chances of a close relationship with the person next to you or finding your mission in professional perspective are huge and almost instantaneous. I am very excited to share this knowledge with you. Even if you do not have a partner, you will quickly find the right one after you reconcile with your parents.

The Letter of Anger is the third part of the ritual. It is important to follow the sequence to get the result.

You have to sit down comfortably and start writing on a piece of paper by pouring all your pain, anger and bad feelings towads your parents in this letter. There is no censoring here. It is very important that you are honest for yourself and to take away all the pain you are holding that was caused by your parents in the process of your bringing up. Each painful moment, each misunderstanding, each pain your parents have caused you consciously or unconsciously must come out from your soul and pour on a piece of paper. Do not be kind and careful here, but just be honest. You may call your parents bad words in this letter. It is very important that your pain is all poured down on the paper. This letter is for you only. It will not be given to your parents. A separate letter shall be written for your mother, father, brother, sister, husband, wife. What you do here is a personal process and you do not share it with anyone!

This part of the ritual is related to the following:

Take the letter you have written and burn it by saying the following words:

> "Let the fire burn the evil between us and i am inviting the good, the love and the warmth in my life and my relationship to come,To be removed from me. I do it with respect and honour. Let the fire turn it into ashes and become something new. ". I do it with all my respect and honour ". Words are spoken aloud as the fire is burning the letter.

When the letter is all burned, gather the ashes. Then you must go to a place where there is a forest or flower garden, and scatter the ashes by saying aloud, "Let the wind and the earth scatter the ashes, accept them and let the new come into my life".

Fourth part of the ritual: Writing the Good Letter

The Good Letter is written and sent to your parents, your beloved man or woman, aswell as to your brother and/or sister, the people in the family with whom you have a difficult relationship. This ritual is mostly done for you so that love can come into your life and you reconcile with your family on a spiritual level. Then you have completely finished your part.

As I said earlier, sometimes relatives have to be loved from a distance. And very often the bad attitude towards us is a perverse and confused way of expressing their love. We can only take care of us and our children, but when we are at peace with ourselves and our parents on a spiritual level, we allow ourselves to be truly loved, happy and successful in our lives. There is no exception for anyone here. Unlike the Letter of Anger which remains for us, this letter must be sent to our parents and relatives with whom we want to have good relations.

It is structured so that it touches the most important strings of the soul and reconciles souls at the energy level. Please do not expect an instant result as a feedback. People will respond according to their level of development and the ability to give love. For sure, I know from my experience that there will be huge results for you and your present family.

My practice shows that there is a 100% positive result for your present family. After this ritual a partner will enter your life, children will be born with ease and love will come into your life. There are no exceptions if the ritual is performed by following the steps. 90% of people begin to communicate with their parents at the parent-child level and feel full satisfaction. We must never forget the Laws of Love in our lives, if we want to live well here on earth. And now the last part of the ritual for you, dear readers.

The Good Letter is written by hand, on a piece of paper, and is sent by mail to whom it is intended for or is given personally in an envelope. It is not read in your presence, but when the person is alone in order to understand the words.

5.4. The Good Letter

Dear mom/dad,

If you have not heard from your parents long ago, you can write: (It's been a long time. I have been thinking about you and I wanted to meet you. There are so many things we can say to each other so that we meet again.)

What I like in you as a man / woman is........

What I value in you as a person is....

What I respect in you as a father / mother is...

What I have always wanted to tell you is...

What I have to confess to you as a secret is....

I want you to become my father / mother again. To build our relationship again, to get to know each other with the time that remains for us as a father and daughter, a father, and a son, etc.

What I have been afraid of as a child was...

What I'm afraid of now is that we will not be close.

What I would like to thank you for is....

What I'm asking you to forgive me is...

What I forgive you for is...

What I want to experience with you from now on is that we meet. You hug me. We talk to each other; you give me advice. We have the possibility to tell each other everything we have not done so far.

Dear Father / Mother, thank you for my life. For choosing to have me as your child.

I accept every part of what has happened to us. That was our path in life. But what I know is that you and I are still standing on that path. And we can meet again. I feel love for you that I have not expressed yet. Please give me a chance to show it to you. I miss you and I hope we meet again. I carry you with all my respect and honour in my heart because I have healed the pain. I need my father / mother beside me. I recognize you. I bow before your power and your genus.

Your daughter / son,

.... your name

This letter is written individually for each person by strictly following the steps.

It is sent personally, on paper, not by e-mail, to the person for whom it is intended for.

It takes some time for this letter to be understood and accepted, but it always has a positive result for us. If our parents are not among the living, the ritual is performed as if they were before us. A letter is written, then it is burned, or the Good Letter can be read aloud at the grave of the parent with respect to their destiny.

These exercises, given in the book, will completely change your life in just one month if you do them subsequently. I recommend some prayers to protect you and your family. I have personally experienced their huge result. Please read them every day when you wake up and whatever happens, it will turn for good. These prayers are accepted everywhere. They have the power to protect you and open the doors for you. These prayers are structured to protect our aura and body from bad influences and thoughts.

6. Prayers and formulas for attracting love, abundance, harmony and personal protection for success in our lives

The Good Prayer:

Dear Lord, our blessed and heavenly father,

Who has given us life and health to rejoice you.

Please send your spirit to protect and guard us from all the evil and cunning thoughts.

Teach us to do your will, to enlighten your name and to praise you always.

Enlighten our spirit, enlighten our hearts and minds, to keep your commandments and statutes.

Inspire in us with your presence your pure thoughts and guide us to serve you with joy.

Bless our life, which we dedicate to you, for the good of our brothers and neighbours.

Help us to grow in every knowledge and wisdom, to learn from your word and abide in your truth.

Lead us in everything we think and do for your name to be for the success of your kingdom on earth.

Feed our souls with your heavenly bread, strengthen us with your power, to succeed in our lives.

By giving us all your blessings, give us your love, to be our eternal law. For to you belongs the Kingdom, the Power, and the Glory for ever.

Amen!

Psalm 23 and 91 of the Bible have powerful effect to protect us, read them every day.

Psalm 22, Psalm of David and Psalm 90

Morning Prayer for Every Day:

Dear Lord, bless my soul! Thank you for waking up today to do my work as it should be done, wherever I am and I may grow as much as I need.

Amen!

Formulas to use in times of great difficulties for clearing your path and attracting the good in your life

When a man and a woman have a quarrel, we say out loud 20 times:
Love and Consent

God lives in you, you are good!
(With these words you overcome bad people.)

When you want to succeed in work, you say out loud every day, three times:
Inspiration, Inspiration, Inspiration.

When you need faith, you will say:
Dear Lord, fill me with faith!

When you need love, you will say:
Dear Lord, unite me with Love!

Blow and say:
H-O-O, Free me, Lord, from bad thoughts and free my soul!

7. Invaluable tips for a harmonious and loving bond between a man and a woman in a relationship/marriage

1. The woman always sleeps on the left side of the man without exception. You will ask, "Why?" Because the left side is related to femininity, and the right side is related to strength. So, you are loving by nature, and you activate the strength and success in man on a physical level. Moreover, you always sit and eat on the left side of the man.

2. When the man comes back from work, kiss him gently and leave him alone for 30 minutes. After that, he will be open to you and will listen to you. The man needs time to switch from work to rest, give him this time.

3. Do not say bad things about your husband's parents and his other relatives. If you are saying bad things about them, you exclude them from the family system at the energy level thus creating the prerequisite for your child to represent them, the excluded relatives, with their actions - to be a difficult child, sick, etc. By saying bad things about them, you do so that the family behind you has difficulties. Take these people as they are and live your life. This is very important for you to have a good relationship.

4. In general principle, if you have not corrected your relationships with your parents, you will be facing a difficult father-in-law and mother-in-law. There are no exceptions here. That's why it is so important to be at peace with our parents in order to have a happy life.

5. We are not looking for dating married people, we deserve love. We work with our mother in a constellation, if we are looking for impossible relationships at subconscious level. This is not ours, but this is an entanglement with the women in the family. There is a way out of this situation with constellation to have a good and loving monogamous connection.

6. We do not lie to the man beside us because it will build walls between us.

7. We practice sports and eat healthy food, even if no one in our family does it.

8. We drink water. A very important point for us so that we are not nervous, and we do not have a short temper.

9. We choose our friends- positive people with goals in life and we stay away from people with addictions and those complaining all the time.

10. We read books. One does not learn everything from their parents, there is information that will help us. We do not become desperate and low-spirited, but we seek. There is always a solution to every situation.

11. We do not obsess the man with our emotional problems, but we solve them. Our husband is not our father. Mature people solve their own emotional problems by themselves. We do not threaten, insult and hurt to get attention. Such behaviour is inherent to children, not to mature people.

12. We do not offend our parents; we do not live with them after we reach 20 years of age. We do not preach to them, but accept them as they are. They are just human beings and have the right to live their lives as they like, like a man and a woman.

13. We do not interfere with interpersonal; family dispu... and we keep neutrality, we never take sides.

14. We do not interfere with our children's lives. They are personalities and have their separate path in life. We respect their fate and their choice.

15. First, we take care of ourselves. Then, we take care for our husband/wife, and after that for the children. There is hierarchy in the family. Children never stand before parents, but after them because they are children and they are not equal. Children must never

witness a dispute between their parents. If this happens, they should go to another room. Children never have to choose between mother and father. They should be able to love their parents equally, we should never bring our children into conflict, even in case of divorce. Relations between parents do not affect children.

16. To have a complete relationship, it is very important that partners have good sex. We need to find time for this. We are not just friends; above all we are two persons loving each other. That is why sex is important in a relationship.

17. We make compliments to each other and we thank each other. We have to understand that the other partner is not obliged to us for anything. We thank for everything we receive in our relationship from the person beside us, even if it is something small. When we give more, we stimulate the other partner to give more too. There is an exchange in the relationship and both partners go together, beside each other, happy.

18. We always stand behind our husband. We never humiliate him in front of other people or children, we keep his back.

19. We do not forget anniversaries and we always pay efforts to look nice and beautiful for our husband.

20. We cook for our husband and children at least at weekends.

21. We must find a goal in our life and we have to follow it, however small and insignificant it may seem to us. We are above all a unique personality with our own interests. We choose something we love to do, something that makes us happy, apart from our children and husband.

8. How do we know what partner we want and if he is the right person for us?

Dear readers, I am giving you this knowledge because I want the best for you, my readers. This method is very accurate and is in full compliance with what we want and we long to get from the man/ woman beside us. It has been used since ancient times in Tibet. One of my teachers was so good at teaching me this technique. And you know what? Everything we have wanted is surprisingly activated. Especially if you strictly follow the instructions given here in this book.

Part One

You must sit down alone when there is nobody near you and you close your eyes. You imagine two ex important sexual partners for you. Please, take an hour for each of them. Do not do it at the same time.

You start with your first ex partner. You take a sheet of paper and write down the name of the person. Divide the sheet of paper into two parts by a vertical line. Write plus and minus in each column. The left column will be minus, and the right one will be plus. You start with the left column. Write only in the left column now. Describe 15 negative qualities that have been very irritating to you and which your partner has shown in your relationship. You do this for both partners. For each partner you must use a new sheet of paper. Please be as honest as possible and do not justify your partner if he was aggressive or if he lied to you. You must write it down. It is important to be honest with yourself so that a new and better partner enters your life. It is very interesting, but when we do this, your current partner, if you have one, will start to change for good.

In order to achieve an effect, you must not share with friends, mothers, your relatives. This is your life and only you can call the happiness. Do not sabotage it with unnecessary disclosure. Learn to keep your affairs just for you.

When you are ready, you take two sheets of paper and put them side by side. Watch them.

In the minuses, was there anything that annoyed you and suggested that this partner was not for you? Select a total of 15 negative qualities from the two sheets of paper and write them down on a new sheet of paper that has no name. Divide it again by a vertical line, typing again plus and minus in each column. On the new sheet of paper, in the minus column write down the total of 15 bad qualities of the two ex partners which were most irritating for you. When you write them down, start turning them into a plus. For example:

1. He is arrogant. In the Plus column you write down - gentle

2. He is irresponsible. In the Plus column you write down – responsible.

You do this until you turn all the minuses into pluses.

When you are ready and you have all the pluses, you copy them to a new sheet of paper, just the pluses. You must throw away the other sheets of paper.

At the top of the plus sheet, you write down

My beloved man is....

This is the man you need now, and this is what you are looking for. You put this sheet of paper on a visible place, and you read it every day for three months so your consciousness can get used it and attract such a man into your life. Even if you have a man in your life, if you follow the advice described above in the book for three months, then your man/woman will become exactly as you want him/her.

I recommend that each reader go through a constellation for the birth family because all traumas that we carry come from the family. Then you have to work for a man and for a present family. From my experience, I know that this works the best way possible - always and for everyone.

Why do men have problems with the woman beside them?

Very often, men have problems with the women beside them because of untreated traumas that relate to their mothers or grandmothers. Sometimes, such traumas are unconscious and get projected on the partners, e.g. aggression, adultery, and physical abuse. In such cases, we should work with the mothers in constellation and everything will fall into place. Very often, when the mother is a powerful woman, the son stands beside her as a spiritual spouse and there is no room for another woman to stand beside him. The same entanglement often occurs when the father is more timid and stands second. That is, the son does not associate with the male part through his father but connects with himself through the mother, which is detrimental to the man. I guess, many of you were in relationships where everything was good at first, but then it turned out you were one too many because the mother acted as a girlfriend's competitor. This is fixed in constellation and the son takes his place as a son in the system and not as an emotional husband. Only then can he have a real relationship with the woman beside him. Do not hurry to separate before going through a constellation.

A mother can manipulate her son by saying "Nobody will love you more than me, I understand you about everything, I forgive you all ... No one else will be able to love you". It is difficult for a man to succeed in such as case as the mother holds him tight to her apron strings, creating in him a sense of responsibility and guilt.

A mother who truly loves her son will give him freedom and not stand in his way. She will stay second, after his girlfriend or wife, to be his support.

In the family system, according to family constellations, when our children have their own families, we parents stand behind them – the mother on the left, the father on the right - so that they can lean on us in difficult moments, without us pushing them into the direction we want.

If this system breaks, our children will never have a happy life or marriage. They will only have what we think is happiness for them. However, our vision of their happiness will destroy their identity.

Why do women have problems with the men beside them?

Women who have problems with the men beside them often play emotional support for their mothers (father is missing, divorce, father died early). Also, very often, mothers get tainted and their daughters stand by their fathers. They become their favourites, that is, they take the place of their mothers or grandmothers if they live with their grandparents. This happens because, in the field of knowledge, everyone has a place and if one is entangled, another gets entangled there to keep the energy running. Children do this from deep unconscious loyalty to their parents just because they received their lives from them. They are even ready to sacrifice their own happiness for their kind and parents.

It is very difficult for people to be really happy when their families have many problems. This can only happen if there is constellation and the problems and burdens return to those to whom they belong.

Unfortunately, tricks never work for good relationships. This can only happen if everyone takes their place in the family system, both children and parents. Then, the energy of love will flow freely between the members of the system.

Why do women have problems with their mothers-in-law?

Women who have good partners, but bad mothers-in-law often had a very traumatic childhood and were deprived of true love and support by their mothers. Also, their mothers could have been physically ill and, thus, the girls had to become their emotional mothers, or the mothers could have been divorced and their children had to take up the role of their partners by giving them emotional support. All this is unconscious but has serious consequences in the relationships with other people. With constellation and inner work with the mothers, this can be fixed. The connection between a man and a woman is enhanced by their children, whether alive or not, by miscarriage and abortion or the early death of a child. Abortion almost always leads to the end of a relationship. If the couple wants to stay together, it is important that the miscarried or aborted child be specially honoured by both parents and a place for it be found in the heart of each parent. An abortion is not completely fixed if parents do not mourn for their child and not consider it loss and death. Only then does the relationship have a chance to revive.

How can we have no problems in our relationships? Important information for each of us!

Growth means taking responsibility for ourselves by staying children to our parents and grandparents. This means always remembering that we are their children and have no right and are not capable of resolving the emotional problems of our parents. We can have a happy relationship with our partners only if we remain children to our parents. Both partners must take the responsibility for the relationship because a good relationship is possible only after each partner accepts their parents exactly as they are, without any claims or objections to them. Acceptance of parents becomes a fact when we admit that, along with all the good things, we have inevitably received not so good things from them, too. Acceptance of parents sometimes takes long time. The process may take longer, but only after that acceptance people are able to experience love, to be healthy, have a very successful business or career, and pass on adequately to their children.

9. The tree of wishes

Let us talk about the tree of our wishes. I call it this way because it is alive, and we can increase what we want if we feed our thoughts the right way. Please do as follows:

First, make a board of your wishes. It is very simple. To make it, you will need a large sheet of cardboard sized about 50 x 50 cm. Take pens, pencils, and various magazines.

At the top of the sheet, write your name in capital letters - like a book title – and the year. For example: Zornitsa 2018

Then, in your thoughts, divide it into four parts. The upper two parts are your personal and sexual life. The lower two parts are your career and money. Start filling in these parts with drawings and clippings from the magazines. Do not be modest in your demands but want boldly from the Universe. Remember, everything must correspond to the qualities you possess. You can include a picture of the last BMW model or a large house with a yard. Think seriously about how you imagine yourself being married, with children, in a monogamous relationship. It is important to be specific in what you want to get. My card became a fact in 8 months. Now I want the same for you - my clients and readers. Please be brave and honest. Only you will have access to the card. When you are done, hang it on the wall, somewhere in the house where you live, so that you can see it. Watch it for at least 10 minutes a day. Very soon, you will see your wishes coming true one by one. I recommend you to write all your wishes on a sheet of paper and consider them first as the universe does not know what is good or bad for you, it just fulfils. Dream boldly on your card. It will be very interesting to me if you share on my page how your wishes have been materializing.

The second thing you need to do is lie down each day, relax, and imagine that you already have what you want. THOUGH IN DE-

TAILS, TRYING TO SENSE IT. For example, you are surfing with your husband. Imagine how you go to Hawaii each year, bathe in the ocean, and have fun with your husband. Imagine how you watch the sunset from the hotel, which is 5 stars, how you lie on the beach. Imagine everything in detail. Be specific, this is important.

If you are alone and want a man or woman in your life to appear, let us make some changes to your home. Let us invite him or her to come to you. Start with the bed. Put two pillows as if your beloved is already there. It is very important not to live in the past but here and now.

The next step is - however small your bedroom may be - placing the bed so that two people can walk on both sides. That is, only the frame where the head rests should touch a wall. This is important in order for you to be able to prepare on the spiritual level that there will be another in your life. Remove any photos of you alone. Put a picture of a loving couple, a man and a woman, to attract the same into your life.

It is important to do so. What is more, if there are any metal objects or mirrors, they must be removed from the bedroom because they act negatively on love, especially mirrors.

10. Parental Blessing – the seminar that will change your life here and now

I organize this seminar several times a year.

Very often, we as children hold a deep insult to our parents. We often forget that they are a man and a woman, not just parents, and have the right to live their lives the way they want just like us.

Parental Blessing is a seminar with constellations. It is a deep, internal process in which "gaps are filled" and the people excluded from the system occupy their exact places. You, as children, leave completely free of old patterns and miracles begin to happen in your life as the love channel starts to flow freely. This is a deep, group meditative constellation, with a powerful healing and therapeutic effect for a better, harmonious, and filled with love and material benefits life. And the most important part is that we treat the traumas. Your mother and father take their place in your heart and everything is happening with ease in your life. My life has changed radically after such a ritual, and I want the best for you - my clients and readers – here and now.

More information about the event can be found on my site: www.zornitsamaleva.com

11. How to love myself, my parents, and the man beside me healthily?

How to love myself?

Write down 10 things, which you are proud of and start with:

1. I AM A GOOD PERSON ....
2. ....
3. ....
4. ....
5. ....
6. ....
7. ....
8. ....
9. ....
10. ....

Write down 10 wonderful things about your mother which you are proud of:

1. My mother is a wonderful mother because.......
2.
3.
4.
5.
6.
7.
8.
9.
10.

Write down 10 wonderful things about your father which you are proud of:

1.
2.
3.
4.
5.
6.
7.
8.
9.
10.

Write down 10 wonderful things about your beloved man which you are proud of:

1. My beloved man hugs me every day
2.
3.
4.
5.
6.
7.
8.
9.
10.

Write down 10 wonderful things about your beloved woman which you are proud of:

1. My beloved woman kisses me for good morning every day.
2.
3.
4.
5.
6.
7.
8.
9.
10.

Please write down 10 things you would like to have in your relationship by starting with

1. I make passionate sex 4 times a week with my beloved partner.
2. I have ....
3.
4.
5.
6.
7.
8.
9.
10.

Affirmations for women:

I love with all my heart my beloved man.

I believe my husband is strong and can handle everything.

For me, my husband is important.

Requesting something from man

I am sitting down on the left side of the man and in a soft and gentle voice I tell him only once, what I want him to do or give me – I do not scream and do not repeat.

I receive everything with ease.

When you have hard times, repeat these affirmations:

"Men are a bit slower and need time to think and reconsider before they do or give anything. They do not like to be treated as children and you must not insist immediately and at the moment".

When you want something, ask for it a day or two before the deadline in order to receive it and always thank for that.

We should never forget that no one is obliged to us and we have a father.

Please do not forget the Laws of Love in order to have a harmonious mutual relation.

When you have difficult moments with the man beside you, write down immediately 10 things that he has done for you today. For example:

He made me coffee, he kissed me, etc. However small they are, they are important. You'll be surprised at how much your man is doing for you every day.

1.

2.

3.

4.

5.

6.

When you have difficult moments with the woman beside you, write down immediately 10 things that she has done for you today. For example:

She made me coffee, she kissed me, etc. However small they are, they are important. You'll be surprised at how much your man is doing for you every day.

1.

2.

3.

4.

5.

6.

My plan for my life:

WITHIN ONE WEEK I WILL DO ......

1.

2.

3.

4.

5.

6.

7.

8.

9.

10.

WITHIN ONE MONTH I WILL DO......

1.

2.

3.

4.

5.

6.

7.

8.

9.

10.

WITHIN THREE MONTHS I WILL DO......

1.

2.

3.

4.

5.

6.

7.

8.

9.

10.

WITHIN ONE YEAR I WILL DO......

1.

2.

3.

4.

5.

6.

7.

8.

9.

10.

WITHIN FIVE YEARS I WILL DO....

1.

2.

3.

4.

5.

6.

7.

8.

9.

10.

WITHIN TEN YEARS I WILL HAVE

1.

2.

3.

4.

5.

6.

7.

8.

9.

10.

I AM HAPPY BECAUSE I HAVE

1.

2.

3.

4.

5.

6.

7.

8.

9.

10.

11.

12.

13.

14.

15.

16.

Write 10 things you are grateful for starting with:

TODAY I AM SO HAPPY AND GRATEFUL THAT **I HAVE NOW.....**

1.
2.
3.
4.
5.
6.
7.
8.
9.
10.

TODAY I WILL DO ....

1.
2.
3.
4.
5.
6.
7.
8.
9.
10.

THESE ARE SOME OF THE AFFIRMATIONS THAT CHANGED MY LIFE AND NOW I GIVE THEM TO YOU ...

YOU MUST READ THEM EVERY DAY FOR 1 YEAR, THEN EACH WEEK, FOR LIFE.

I love what I work, and I get paid very well for that.

Or, I have very successful business with very satisfied and loyal customers around the world and I attract new and new customers and my profits are doubled each month.

I am a happy woman, I am loved by my parents and supported by them. They are healthy and they can take care of themselves, so I can concentrate on my loving family and my work which I adore and have good income. I have a fantastic, generous and loving, monogamous and supportive husband, healthy and happy children.

12. Who am I?

Hi I am ....
....
....
....
....
....
....
....
....
....
....

Thank you for reading this book....

The change for you has already started here and now...

Yours Zornitsa – (Amira)

Sources

1. Bert Hellinger – The Laws of Love – Overview How to Make Love Happen, "Zhana 98-Publishing House".

2. Bert Hellinger – Spiritual Family Conservation – Obzor, "Zhana 98-Publishing House".

3. Indra Torsten Preiss – The Method of Family Constellations – Institute of Art and Therapy-Sofia-2016.

4. The Five Languages of Love – Gary Chapman – Nov Vek Publishing House – Sofia-2016.

5. Bertold Ulsamer – The Healing Power of the Past – Anand Publishing House-2014.

6. The Bible – New Testament.

Parental Blessing

Zornitsa Maleva

First edition, English, 2023
Publisher: Zornitsa Maleva

Cover illustration: Mira Doichinova
Prepress: Katerina Valkova
Editor: Snezhina Tsvetanova
Editor on English: Vaniya Angelova
Print: Direct Services Ltd.

ISBN: 978-619-92596-0-3